W9-BFN-762

UNSUNG HEROES
OF THE SUPER BOWL

by Paul Bowker

12 STORY LIBRARY

www.12StoryLibrary.com

12-Story Library is an imprint of Bookstaves.

Photographs ©: Allen Kee/Associated Press, cover, 1; Vernon J. Biever/Associated Press,
4; Debby Wong/Shutterstock.com, 5; Focus on Sport/Getty Images, 6; dean bertoncelj/
Shutterstock.com, 7; Associated Press, 8; dean bertoncelj/Shutterstock.com, 9; Al
Messerschmidt/Associated Press, 10; Focus on Sport/Getty Images, 12; dean bertoncelj/
Shutterstock.com, 13; Bob Galbraith/Associated Press, 14; John Gaps III/Associated Press,
16; dean bertoncelj/Shutterstock.com, 17; Morry Gash/Associated Press, 18; Katherine
Welles/Shutterstock.com, 19; Scott Boehm/Associated Press, 20; Elaine Thompson/
Associated Press, 22; Ted Kerwin/CC2.0, 23; Kevin Terrell/Associated Press, 24; You Touch
Pix of EuToch/Shutterstock.com, 25; Ric Tapia/Associated Press, 26; sv1ambo/CC2.0, 28;
Toca Marine/Shutterstock.com, 29

ISBN
978-1-63235-548-5 (hardcover)
978-1-63235-666-6 (ebook)

Library of Congress Control Number: 2018947548

Printed in the United States of America
Mankato, MN
June 2018

Access free, up-to-date content on this
topic plus a full digital version of this book.
Scan the QR code on page 31 or use your
school's login at 12StoryLibrary.com.

Table of Contents

Matt Snell Is Super Runner

In 1969, New York Jets quarterback Joe Namath got the fame. He guaranteed a victory for the Jets in Super Bowl III. He backed up his mighty words. Namath passed for 206 yards. He was not intercepted. He directed the Jets to a 16-7 victory over the Baltimore Colts. Namath was named game MVP.

Matt Snell was the workhorse. He was given the ball 30 times. He scored the only touchdown for the Jets in the second quarter on a run of four yards. The touchdown made Super Bowl history. Snell ran around the left end for a Jets touchdown. It gave New York a lead of 7 to 0.

It marked the first time that a team from the American Football League defeated a team from the National Football League in a Super Bowl. Snell did not get the fame. But the running back played a big part in the Jets upset victory over the Colts. Years later, for unknown reasons, he would refuse to participate in a Jets Ring of Honor ceremony.

Players attend a Ring of Honor ceremony.

JUST FOR KICKS

Matt Snell scored the touchdown. Jim Turner made the kicks. Turner kicked three field goals for the New York Jets in Super Bowl III. The field goals helped the Jets become the first American Football League team to win the Super Bowl. Turner had field goals of 32, 30, and 9 yards. They provided the winning points in the victory by the Jets..

121
Yards run by Matt Snell in Super Bowl III.

- Quarterback Joe Namath was named game MVP.
- Running back Snell scored the only touchdown of the game for New York.
- The Jets became the first AFL team to win the Super Bowl.

Chuck Howley Is Unique MVP

Chuck Howley had a terrific game in Super Bowl V in 1971. He made two interceptions. He recovered a fumble. And he was named Super Bowl MVP. He did not have something that every other Super Bowl MVP had. Howley and his teammates did not have a championship trophy to bring back home. His team, the Dallas Cowboys, lost to the Baltimore Colts. Howley became the only member of a losing team to ever win the MVP of the Super Bowl.

The Colts scored 10 points in the final quarter to get the victory. The teams combined for 11 turnovers

3

Number of interceptions Chuck Howley made in two Super Bowl games.

- Howley is the only player of a losing Super Bowl team to be named game MVP.
- Howley had two interceptions and a fumble recovery in Super Bowl V.
- Dallas Cowboys lost to the Baltimore Colts by a score of 16-13.
- The game featured 11 turnovers.

in the game. Cowboys quarterback Craig Morton was intercepted three times. The Cowboys also lost the ball on a fumble. Howley recovered three of the turnovers from Baltimore. It was a special defensive performance. And why Howley was named MVP.

There were reports that Howley refused to accept the award because the Cowboys lost the game. However, he said later in an interview that it wasn't true. He did accept the award. There was not a presentation after the game. Howley was in the showers when he was told about the MVP award.

Robert Newhouse Achieves Fullback Perfection

The play didn't call for a run. The play didn't call for a punishing block. It did call for an accurate throw by Dallas Cowboys fullback Robert Newhouse. The trick play turned into a highlight for Super Bowl XII in 1978. Newhouse delivered a touchdown pass of 29 yards to Golden Richards. It came in the fourth quarter. It was the final clinching blow. The Cowboys won by a score of 27-10 against the Denver Broncos.

158.3

The passer rating for Dallas Cowboys fullback Robert Newhouse in Super Bowl XII. This is the highest rating that can be achieved.

- Newhouse threw a touchdown pass to Golden Richards in the final quarter.
- The fullback also rushed for fifty-five yards.
- The Cowboys defeated the Denver Broncos by a score of 27-10.
- Newhouse played in three Super Bowl games for the Cowboys.

DOUBLE THE MVPS

Two Super Bowl MVPs were named during Super Bowl XII. The only time in history. Harvey Martin and Randy White led the Dallas Cowboys defense in their win over the Denver Broncos. Martin had two sacks. White had one sack. They forced eight turnovers. Denver Broncos quarterback Craig Morton was intercepted four times. The Broncos lost four fumbles.

Cowboys coach Tom Landry would later say it was the play that won the game for Dallas. Newhouse was a fullback. He was often a blocking back for Cowboys running back Tony Dorsett. Cowboys quarterback Roger Staubach pitched the ball back to Newhouse on the scoring play. Newhouse started running to the left. Then he stopped. He tossed the ball downfield to Richards. The game was the second of three Super Bowls that Newhouse played in. The touchdown pass was the only pass he threw in three Super Bowl games.

4

John Stallworth Is Record Receiver

In 1980, Pittsburgh Steelers John Stallworth had an iconic moment in Super Bowl XIV. He was running a deep pass route. He looked back over his shoulder for a pass thrown by Steelers quarterback Terry Bradshaw. Stallworth caught it over the arms of Rams defender Rod Perry. He kept running with the ball. It turned into a touchdown play covering 73 yards. It was just one of the scoring plays for the Steelers. They defeated the Rams by a score of 31-19.

Bradshaw won the Super Bowl MVP award for the second year in a row. He passed for two touchdowns and 309 yards. He also was MVP of Super Bowl XIII in 1979. The Steelers defeated the Cowboys in that game.

Stallworth is one of the Pittsburgh receivers who made all that happen. He scored the Steelers first two touchdowns in the game. He caught three passes for 115 yards.

The next year he caught three passes for 121 yards. And he scored one touchdown in Super Bowl XIV. Stallworth set a Super Bowl record in Super Bowl XIV. He averaged 40.3 yards per catch. And won his fourth Super Bowl ring in Super Bowl XIV. He also set a Super Bowl record by averaging 24.4 yards per catch in four Super Bowl games.

14

Number of seasons John Stallworth played for the Pittsburgh Steelers, from 1974 through 1987.

- Stallworth averaged more than forty yards per catch in Super Bowl XIV.
- Stallworth set a Super Bowl record in average yards per catch. He set records for a single Super Bowl game and Super Bowl career.
- He caught two touchdown passes in Super Bowl XIII, one touchdown pass in Super Bowl XIV.

11

Rod Martin Is Interception King

Rod Martin sealed the deal late in Super Bowl XV. Martin was a linebacker for the Oakland Raiders. He had already intercepted two passes to tie a Super Bowl record. Martin intercepted a third pass with three minutes left in the 1981 game. It was the final big play in a game the Raiders won by a score of 27-10. They defeated the Philadelphia Eagles.

Martin went to work early in the game. He intercepted Eagles quarterback Ron Jaworski on the third play run of the game by the Philadelphia offense. The interception set up a touchdown drive for the

THINK ABOUT IT

The Super Bowl record of three interceptions by Rod Martin is remarkable. No other player has had more than two interceptions in a Super Bowl since that game. What makes the achievement even more noteworthy is that Martin was a linebacker. He was not a defensive back. Do you think his record will continue to stand? What will it take to beat it?

12

Draft round that Oakland Raiders selected Rod Martin in 1977.

- Martin intercepted Eagles quarterback Ron Jaworski three times.
- Raiders quarterback Jim Plunkett was named the game MVP.
- Martin got his first interception of the day on the third offensive play run by the Eagles.

Raiders. Martin got his second interception in the third quarter. His three-time interception record still stands more than 36 years later.

Martin was the defensive star in Super Bowl XV. He was not selected MVP of the game. That honor went to Raiders quarterback Jim Plunkett. Martin kept all three balls at his home after retiring.

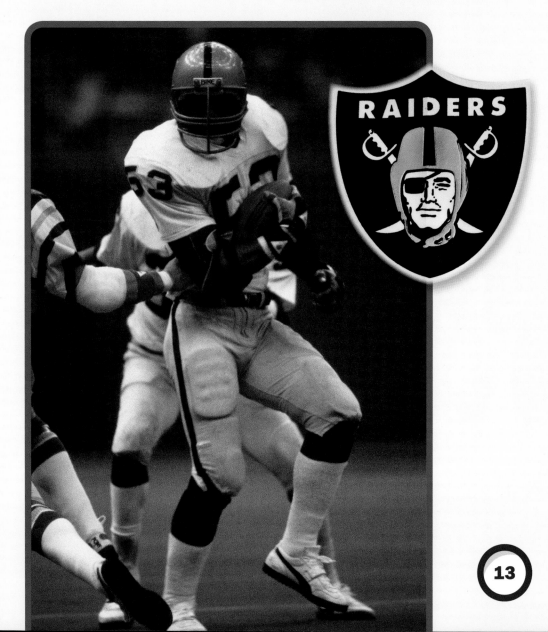

Timmy Smith Makes Amazing Rookie Start

Timmy Smith had never started a game for the Washington Redskins. He was a rookie running back in 1987. He played in seven games during the regular season. He had never scored a touchdown. That all changed in Super Bowl XXII. Smith was told just prior to the 1988 game that he would be starting. Smith delivered in a big way for the Redskins. He rushed for a Super Bowl record of 204 yards. He scored two touchdowns.

The Redskins blew away the Denver Broncos. The Redskins won the game by a score of 42-10.

Another star of the day was Redskins quarterback Doug Williams. He became the first black quarterback to win a Super Bowl. Williams was named Super Bowl MVP.

WASHINGTON WORKHORSES

Timmy Smith was a workhorse for the Washington Redskins in Super Bowl XXII. He had 22 carries in the game. Redskins running back John Riggins did even better five years earlier. Riggins had 38 carries in Super Bowl XVII. He rushed for 166 yards and one touchdown. The Redskins won both games.

22
Number of carries by Timmy Smith in Super Bowl XXII.

- Smith was a rookie in the NFL. He made his first pro start in Super Bowl XXII.
- Smith ran for a Super Bowl record of 204 yards in the game.
- It was the only Super Bowl that Smith played in. He was in the NFL for just three seasons.

Mike Jones Makes Winning Tackle

Mike Jones had the biggest tackle of his life in Super Bowl XXXIV. He clinched a win for the St. Louis Rams in the 2000 game. Jones stopped Kevin Dyson of the Tennessee Titans on the final play of the game. The tackle came one yard short of the end zone. It gave the Rams the victory by a score of 23-16. Jones was in the ninth season of an NFL career that lasted 11 years. The Rams were the third team he played for.

One play turned Jones into a Super Bowl hero. The Rams had taken the lead on a touchdown with less than two minutes remaining. The Titans answered with a long drive. The Titans marched all the way to the St. Louis 10-yard line. Titans quarterback Steve McNair rolled out of pressure on the next play. He located Dyson for a pass at the 5-yard line. Dyson caught the ball. He headed for the end zone. Jones went low for a tackle. He brought Dyson down before he reached the end zone.

SUPER BOWL BROTHERS

Kevin Dyson was not the only one in his family to play in a Super Bowl game. Andre Dyson played in Super Bowl XL with the Seattle Seahawks. Kevin played in two Super Bowls. He played in Super Bowl XXXIV with the Tennessee Titans and in Super Bowl XXXVIII with the Carolina Panthers. The brothers were on the losing end all three times.

19
Number of games that Mike Jones started for the Rams in 1999.

- Jones made the game-saving tackle on the final play of Super Bowl XXXIV.
- He stopped Tennessee receiver Kevin Dyson on the 1-yard line preventing a possible overtime.
- The tackle gave the Rams their first Super Bowl victory in franchise history.

A-Train
Mike Alstott Delivers

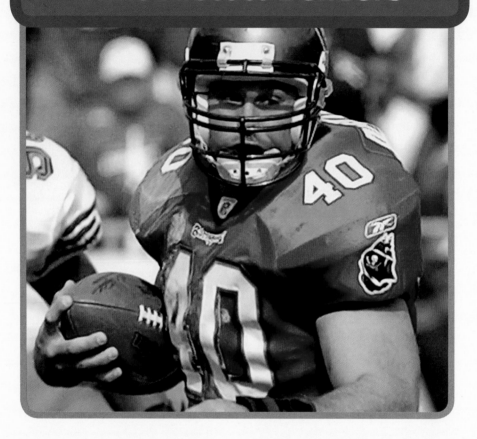

The numbers never told the whole story for fullback Mike Alstott. He rushed for just 15 yards in Super Bowl XXXVII for the Tampa Bay Buccaneers. Alstott still played a huge part in the Bucs winning the 2003 Super Bowl for the first time.

He scored a touchdown to break open a close game in the second quarter. He had 10 rushing attempts. He had many plays in which he was blocking for others. He caught five passes for 43 yards. Alstott was involved in 18 offensive plays as a running back or receiver.

5,088

Rushing yards by Mike Alstott in 12 seasons with the Tampa Bay Bucs.

- Alstott scored a touchdown in Super Bowl XXXVII. And helped Tampa Bay win its first Super Bowl.
- He rushed for 15 yards and 43 receiving yards in the Super Bowl.
- Alstott played a big part in turning the Bucs into a championship team.
- He was a starter from the first game of his rookie season in 1996.

Alstott was later credited by Bucs Vice President Bryan Glazier for helping turn the Bucs from a bad franchise into a championship contender. The Tampa Bay Bucs defeated the Oakland Raiders by a score of 48 to 21. The touchdown scored by Alstott was among 17 points scored in the second quarter by Tampa Bay.

Alstott never played in another Super Bowl. He became known as the A-Train in Tampa. He was one of the most popular players on the Bucs. He retired as the all-time touchdown leader in Bucs franchise history.

Jacoby Jones Returns Longest Kickoff

In 2013, Jacoby Jones of the Baltimore Ravens had already delivered a big play in Super Bowl XLVII. He scored a touchdown on a pass play covering 56 yards. He caught the pass from Ravens quarterback Joe Flacco. He fell to the ground. He got up and ran into the end zone. The play came in the second quarter of the game against the San Francisco 49ers.

Another big play came as the second half of the game began. Jones was back to receive the kickoff from the 49ers. The ball went deep into the end zone. Jones chose to run the ball out. He ran straight through the

THINK ABOUT IT

Jacoby Jones was eight yards deep in the end zone when he caught the kick. Deep kicks are usually downed in the end zone. Would you have run the ball out like Jones did? Or would you have downed it in the end zone?

108

Yards run for touchdowns by kickoff returner Jacoby Jones. It happened three times in his career.

- Jones returned the second half kickoff for a touchdown in Super Bowl XLVII.
- Jones scored another touchdown on a pass play of 56 yards.
- He helped the Baltimore Ravens defeat the San Francisco 49ers by a score of 34-31.

middle of the coverage. He returned the ball all the way for a Ravens touchdown. The kickoff return was a Super Bowl record. It missed being a National Football League record by just one yard. Jones was not selected the game MVP. Flacco received that honor. He passed for 287 yards and three touchdowns.

David Tyree Helmet Catch Leads to Win

New York Giants receiver David Tyree had a bad practice just two days before Super Bowl XLII. He kept fumbling catches. Things changed on the day of the big game in 2008. Tyree made a catch that was one of the best catches in Super Bowl history.

The Giants faced the unbeaten New England Patriots. It was late in the final quarter and they were losing by a score of 14-10. Giants quarterback Eli Manning was under pressure from four Patriots defenders on a third down play. He desperately threw a ball in the direction of Tyree.

CONGRATULATIONS NY GIANTS SUPER BOWL CHAMPIONS!

Tyree got his hands on the ball. He trapped the ball against his helmet. He fell to the ground. He managed to keep the ball secured against his helmet. The catch gave the Giants a first down. Manning passed to Plaxico Burress for a touchdown with 35 seconds remaining.

4

Number of pass catches that David Tyree had in the 2007 season.

- Tyree made an important catch late in Super Bowl XLII. He pinned the ball against his helmet.
- The catch set up a winning touchdown pass from Giants quarterback Eli Manning to Plaxico Burress. It was the final minute of the game.
- Tyree had three catches and scored a touchdown.

UNSUNG SACK ATTACK

The entire Giants team qualified as unsung in 2007. They lost their first two games of the season. They made the playoffs only as a wild card team. The Giants defense rose up in Super Bowl XLII. They sacked Patriots quarterback Tom Brady five times. Justin Tuck sacked Brady twice. A sack by Jay Alford came with 20 seconds left in the game.

11

Dont'a Hightower's Tackle Saves the Game

The biggest hero in Super Bowl XLIX was Malcolm Butler of the New England Patriots. Butler intercepted a Seattle pass on the goal line in the final seconds of the 2015 game. The play rescued a 28-24 victory for the Patriots. Butler became an immediate hero in New England.

But what about the play before the dramatic interception? Seattle running back Marshawn Lynch was stopped one yard short of the end

Hightower makes the tackle on the 1-yard line.

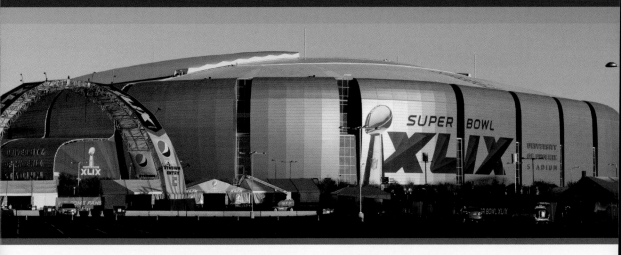

zone by Patriots linebacker Dont'a Hightower. The Seahawks would have won the game if Hightower had not made that tackle. Lynch would have scored a touchdown.

The Seahawks had the ball at the 5-yard line of New England when Hightower made his tackle. Lynch ran to the left side of his offensive line. Hightower was able to fend off his blocker. He got enough of Lynch to send him to the turf just before the goal line. Hightower was able to make the tackle despite playing with a torn labrum. The labrum is attached to the shoulder. Super Bowl history changed on the next play. Lynch was not called on for another running play. The Seahawks instead tried a pass. The ball thrown by Seahawks quarterback Russell Wilson was intercepted by Butler.

Dont'a Hightower won two Super Bowl rings in three years with the Patriots.

7

Number of tackles Dont'a Hightower had in his first two Super Bowls with the New England Patriots.

- Hightower tackled Seattle running back Marshawn Lynch at the one-yard line in the final minute of Super Bowl XLIX.
- The stop by Hightower set up an interception on the next play by Patriots teammate Malcolm Butler.
- Hightower played in the game despite having a shoulder injury.

Julian Edelman Makes Miracle Catch

In 2017, the odds were stacked against the New England Patriots in Super Bowl LI. They trailed the Atlanta Falcons by 25 points in the third quarter.

The Patriots were still behind by eight points in the final minutes of the game. Then Julian Edelman made a catch that defied gravity. Edelman battled three Atlanta

Falcons defenders for a ball thrown by Patriots quarterback Tom Brady. The ball was deflected into the air. Edelman went down with the three Atlanta players. He grabbed the ball before it hit the ground. Inches separated Edelman's hands from the ground. He never let the ball hit the ground. Brady called it one of the best catches he has ever seen.

The Patriots soon scored a touchdown. James White scored it with 50 seconds in regulation. A conversion pass from Brady to Danny Amendola tied the score at 28-28. The Patriots won the game in overtime on another touchdown run by White.

87

Receiving yards that New England Patriots Julian Edelman had in Super Bowl LI.

- Edelman completed a catch just inches above the ground in the final minutes of Super Bowl LI. The play led to a Patriots touchdown.
- Edelman caught the ball after it was tipped into the air by an Atlanta defender and bounced off two players.
- Edelman had five catches in the game and also threw a pass. He earned his second Super Bowl ring with the Patriots victory in overtime.

THINK ABOUT IT

Do you think you could make a catch after the ball was tipped and deflected off two players? What would be the most difficult part of the catch? You would have to keep your balance. You would have to focus on the ball. And keep the ball from touching the ground.

Fun Facts and Stories

Fast and Not So Furious

Chuck Howley of the Dallas Cowboys was named MVP of Super Bowl V despite playing for the losing team. He received a Dodge Charger for winning the award. He did not keep the car for long. It was too much of a sports car for him. Howley later said he did not want to keep a hot rod.

Always a Buc

Mike Alstott always played for the Tampa Bay Bucs. He never played for another team. He won a Super Bowl with them in 2003. So Alstott had tears in his eyes in 2008 when he announced his retirement. Alstott retired as the all-time touchdown leader in Tampa Bay history. He made 71 of them. Alstott said he would miss his teammates the most.

Free Furniture

The kickoff return by Jacoby Jones of the Baltimore Ravens in Super Bowl XLVII produced a bunch of free furniture in Baltimore. Gardiners Furniture is located in Baltimore, Maryland. Leading up to the game, the store promised free furniture if the Ravens scored a touchdown on the opening play. Or the opening play of the second half. Jones opened the second half by scoring a touchdown on a return of 108 yards. The store gave out $600,000 worth of free furniture.

Ball Belongs to Plaxico

The helmet catch of David Tyree in Super Bowl XLII is forever etched into Super Bowl history. The memorable catch set up the winning touchdown for the New York Giants against the New England Patriots. The helmet wound up in the Pro Football Hall of Fame. The ball wound up in the house of Giants receiver Plaxico Burress. The game ball was not switched for another after the catch by Tyree. Burress used the same ball to score his touchdown. So he kept it.

Tennis Balls

New England Patriots receiver Julian Edelman credits tennis balls for his incredible catch in Super Bowl LI. He catches tennis balls thrown off walls to test his reaction. He also ties a hand behind his back and has his sister throw tennis balls at his face. The drill was invented by his dad.

Glossary

franchise

Each team in the National Football League. If the team moves from one city to another, it is still the same franchise.

fullback

An offense player who lines up in the backfield behind the quarterback. They may take the ball on a handoff from the quarterback or go into a blocking position to help another teammate.

interception

When the football is grabbed by a player from the opposing team.

linebacker

A defensive player who is positioned behind the scrimmage line. They make tackles on both running and short passing plays.

MVP

Abbreviation for most valuable player.

overtime

The extra period played if the score is tied at the end of regulation play time.

quarterback

A player who runs the offense. They take the ball on a snap from the center. The quarterback usually passes the ball or hands it off to a running back.

rookie

A first-year player in the National Football League.

running back

A player who lines up in the backfield with the quarterback. Their job is to receive the ball from the quarterback and run with it. Or they may also catch a pass or block for another player who has the ball.

touchdown

When a player with the ball gets into the end zone. A touchdown is worth six points.

turnover

When the defending team gets the ball with an interception or from recovering a fumble.

workhorse

A player who is used often in a game. Such as a running back who is involved in a large number of rushing plays.

For More Information

Books

Howell, Brian, *12 Reasons to Love Football*, Mankato, MN: 12-Story Library, 2018.

Stewart, Mark, *The New York Jets*, Chicago, IL: Norwood House Press, 2013

Kennedy, Mike, *Meet the Cowboys*, Chicago, IL: Norwood House Press, 2011

Nelson, Julie, *New York Giants*, Mankato, MN: Creative Education, 2001

Visit 12StoryLibrary.com

Scan the code or use your school's login at **12StoryLibrary.com** for recent updates about this topic and a full digital version of this book. Enjoy free access to:

- Digital ebook
- Breaking news updates
- Live content feeds
- Videos, interactive maps, and graphics
- Additional web resources

Note to educators: Visit 12StoryLibrary.com/register to sign up for free premium website access. Enjoy live content plus a full digital version of every 12-Story Library book you own for every student at your school.

Index

About the Author

Paul Bowker is an editor and author who lives on Cape Cod in South Yarmouth, Massachusetts. His 35-year newspaper career has included hundreds of NFL games. He is a national past president of Associated Press Sports Editors and has won multiple national writing awards.

32